Healing Through Creative Therapy

Illustrations and Text from a Survivor

JULEE KAI

iUniverse, Inc.
Bloomington

Healing Through Creative Therapy
Illustrations and Text from a Survivor

iUniverse books may be ordered through booksellers or by contacting:

iUniverse
1663 Liberty Drive
Bloomington, IN 47403
www.iuniverse.com
1-800-Authors (1-800-288-4677)

ISBN: 978-1-4502-6215-6 (pbk)
ISBN: 978-1-4502-6216-3 (ebk)

Printed in the United States of America

iUniverse rev. date: 2/4/2011

This compilation of illustrations and text is to help others who have suffered abuse understand that they are not alone. Having been abused physically, verbally, mentally, and sexually plays a huge part in the development of the child. It affects their behavior for their entire life. I call it "living under the influence of abuse."

It is through dedicated, hard work with a competent therapist that recovery is possible. This process can take years. Eventually, one is rewarded by becoming a 'thriver.'

Missy 143

Introduction

As a child I always lived in fear of my father for he was an alcoholic and had periods of extreme rage; throwing things and belting me. I would hide behind a chair. Mother was subjected to his rage as well. Many a dinner would end up on the wall. Foul language and sexual gestures were daily happenings. This was the "norm." He'd also tickle torture and "chew" or gnaw at my body, my chest and belly with his mouth bringing me to tears while tightly holding my arms so I couldn't move.

Many nights I recall mother sitting upstairs with her parents. I was left with father. At times he'd just stand up, take his belt off, and hit me with it. No "warning" words spoken. Then he'd call me a sonofabitch and a fuckin' whore. I was young. Sometimes during the summer he would buy ice cream from the truck at night for both of us. I felt special.

Mother did not believe me when I told her uncle nate was touching my boobies. She disregarded it saying, "You must be mistaken. He wouldn't hurt you. He loves(?) you." So, he continued until I decided not to go to the candy store anymore.

She also told me, "You killed Grandpa. You hurt your knee. He worried about you. He had a heart attack and died." I was ten.

Another uncle would grab my upper arms, bring my chest to his chest, and slide it back and forth. He'd sound an awful moan that resembled his eating his most delicious meal – ever.

My family constantly remarked about my body being top heavy. Brother always laughed.

However, it was only when Ms. Principal "groped" my buttocks at the end of a local Board of Education meeting May 11, 1993, that I immediately began to have flashbacks of being molested. I didn't say anything. I froze. I hoped the floor would open beneath me allowing me to fall through. I did report this the very next morning. I waited until Sunday to tell my husband. I didn't think anyone would listen since no one had before. I began to lose weight. She touched me again during Field Day in June. I entered therapy. During the summer came the first official breakdown. She touched me a third time that same year at Back-to-School Night. She was ordered to stay away from me. I was given an escort from the Board Office if I was to go to the school. Even with that in place she came within one person from me. I had a panic attack. I was in Outpatient now and still losing weight. I had my second official breakdown in April, her contract renewal time. My psychiatrist called me while I was in the hospital telling me she was dropping me because she doesn't treat people like me. I, again, was in Outpatient. Soon, the principal was gone and stability seemed to resume, although I have "roller-coastered" many times since.

My memory began its work. I remember ONLY the "bad" things. This is what you see or read on the following pages. I am told the good memories will come … I'm not sure as to when.

With this summation try to feel for yourself the powers of abuse and understand why all aspects – verbal, physical, sexual, and emotional – must be stopped. To the many of you who have been abused, remember, YOU ARE NOT ALONE. We, survivors, must stand together. Support systems are sometimes difficult to find. They run with denial.

Even with a loving spouse and children the load is heavy. It is a burden to them. Dying seems justified.

With a caring therapist, psychiatrist, other health care professionals and time – lots of time and work – life does begin to change … slowly, ever so slowly.

DISCLOSURE

Always tell someone, anyone,
Always –
            Until someone listens to you.

Do not hold this "secret."
It is his secret, their secret.

Do Not believe you were bad

            My child …

You did Not deserve this.

You are young, vulnerable, and innocent.

He is quite ill.

Take Your life back.

Find the Courage to

            Give Yourself the gift of life and

                        Live it,

                        Enjoy it.

            Laugh, Play, and Sing.

            Find Peace in all Nature surrounding you.

Cry dear child,
Lighten the load,
Feel the pain,
Release the anger.
Lessen your fears.

Allow help from the one whom You disclosed to.

Trust …

BITS AND PIECES

Sometimes the days when I was small
I can't remember them at all.
Wondering why I did not -
I tried to remember but I forgot.

I'd listen while others would speak their recall,
Then wondered why my life's behind walls.
Memories there weren't ready to be found
For no one wanted to hear their sound.

But when it came time in an unusual way
My recall awoke … What did it say?
Yes, all of these things that happened to me
Are very unpleasant, that you can see.

So, here on these pages you'll find in this book
Are bits and pieces of my life. Take a look
At these, the memories I have in my head,
Behavioral patterns – results of problems not said.

They'll be with me forever it's sad to say,
Oh how I wish it would all go away.
My trust and religion have both gone astray,
G-d, why did you do this? I can't even pray.

So, while I am healing it is quite unclear,
But very important my support system is near.
My family, my therapist, and doctors all here
To help make the unbearable able to bear.

I am Different

I am different. In all the world there are others like me. We resemble all others as being human yet others see us as ants or puppets. We used to cry, but not anymore. We used to laugh, but not anymore. We used to care, but not anymore. Now, we wonder why. Why am I like this? Why am I not loved? Why can't I do anything right? Why can't I defend myself? Why am I afraid of the world? Why has being hated, being bad, or being wrong dominated my life? Why am I not equal to others? What's wrong with me? What went wrong in my life? Aren't I special? Am I not deserving of love or a life or freedom without fear? I don't trust – for those who were to protect me abandoned me instead. Others called me bad names or made fun of me; others were allowed to hit me; still others touched me on my torso. I don't feel good about me. I love to draw, but it didn't please them. What I liked didn't matter. It still doesn't.

But now I am different. It is many years later. I will not allow others to treat me like dirt anymore. I am a person. It is time to take a firm stronghold on my life. It is time for me to lift my self-esteem. It is time to remove all negatives in my life whether family, friends, doctors, or employers. It is time to smile, to laugh, to feel, to trust, to love ... but it won't be easy. My pain lies deep, deep inside. The scars will always be there. The abuse and neglect that was given to me will be in my history forever. Now I am aware of its presence in my life and how it has conditioned my behaviors. My body has been numb physically both inside and out; and emotionally as well.

There are parts of me I have never known and parts I've yet to know. Presently, I feel even G-d has abandoned me. "He" should have just deleted me from "His plan." "He" allowed me to be born a victim ... many times over. Now I live a different fear.

I am different. I am a survivor. I will recondition my life. I will become Me, instead of an empty shell. I will feel, smile, laugh, trust, love, and live a little at a time. Yes, I am different.

My support system acknowledges my differences and is helping me to overcome the fear to change. I am different. Physically I am an adult. Emotionally I am a child. Please be tolerant with me as I "grow-up." My life has been like that of a robot ... doing what had to be done without any feelings. Calm to immediate rage, I try not to do that anymore. The new "quiet" scares me. I am trying to take care of me. I am different. I am determined to never become victimized again ... Not me, not my family. Yes, I will take the time it takes to change. At least one dysfunctional family will become a thriving, functional one. Hurdles will be recognized and attacked rather than "shushed" as in the past.

I will be successful. Yes, I am different.

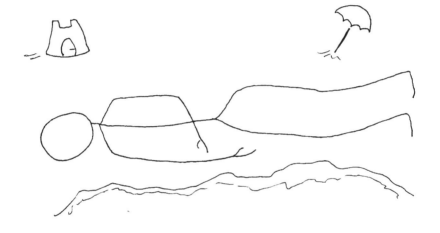

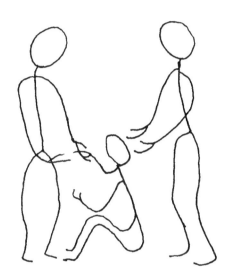

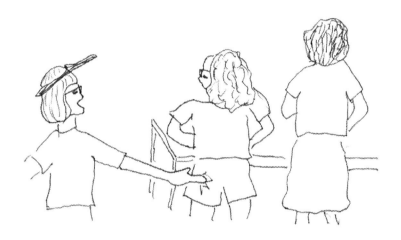

For Candy

Uncle had a candy store attached to his house.
I always felt so lucky. I could have candy anytime I wanted to.

Mother, grandmother, and aunts would not like me
Sitting with them during afternoon visits.
"Go," they would say, "Go see uncle nate..
He will give you candy. He will give you anything you want."
Unknowingly, he could have whatever he wanted to as well.

He would welcome me while sitting upon his stool
At the end of the candy display, in the corner.
It was the only way to get behind the counter and,
Of course, the only way out.

I remember feeling lucky to slide open the doors
Of the counter to choose whatever I felt like having that day.
It was leaving from behind the counter ...

Uncle was still sitting on his stool…
A short, chubby, balding, stubbly bearded-face man
Wearing gray cuffed pants, white button-down shirt,
A belt around his big belly, and eyeglasses.

He sat…with his legs spread wide open.
I would try to pass by him.
With there being no room to leave except to pass by him,
I had no choice.

He would grab hold of me.
He would not let me go.
I wanted him to let me go. He held me tight.
No one else was in the store.

He pulled me up to his body, close, between his legs.
He grabbed me.
He touched my body. He touched my boobies.

I was 10 and I had big girl boobies. How I hated them.
He would make noises as he touched me,

14

As though he was eating something delicious.
I can still hear him.
I can still smell him.
I can still see him there with me.
I don't want to see us anymore.

He held me close, and closer; tight, and tighter.
He was strong. His stubbly face scratched my cheek.
He held my shoulder as he touched me.
I could feel under his pants. I could feel him.
I couldn't get away from him. Still no one else was
in his store.
He breathed on me as he touched me and
touched me.
Still he held me tighter and touched me.
Then, the bell above the door tingled as
A man wearing a hat and long coat came in.
Uncle's tight grip on me fell.
I escaped.
Another time his son walked through
the back door of the store.
He quickly released me then.
I ran.

Yes, I was lucky to have had an uncle who owned a candy store.
He had a sweet, innocent child. He abused
for the arousal of his stiff dick. He was luckier to have had me.
His sexual pleasure was sweeter to him
Than his free candy was to me.

As I walked away from the store,
I see myself as I walked …
As though someone took a movie of me.

I walked one foot on the curb,
One foot on the road
with my head down,
always with my head down.
I didn't want anyone to see me.

He made me feel dirty and bad

As though I did something wrong.
I didn't want to see the store anymore.
I didn't want him to see me.
I didn't want him to reach me to pull me
behind the candy counter anymore.

I see him still. I see him standing outside.
His back up against the window of the store
just next to the receded candy store door.
He stood. His eyeglasses on,
His cigar or pipe in his mouth waiting for me.

I told mother. She was brushing my hair.
She told me, "Who, uncle nate?
He wouldn't hurt you. He loves you."
I was confused. If this is love, I don't love it.
I was a child. I was a sad and lonely child
Who was quite confused.
He fondled me. He molested me. She didn't believe me.
I felt like I didn't matter, that my words were not true.
I thought about telling father, but I knew he would have killed uncle.
I see it.
I feel it.
I will always remember …
how innocent I was, how it felt … always.

Remember what was done to you,
Speak of it, Release the pain,
Surrender to the chains that bind you …
Now I know why.

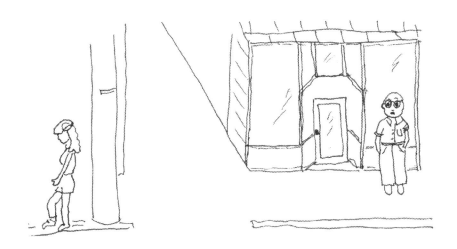

Night Terror

As a child I was aware that I repeatedly had a terrible nightmare. It took place in an old store across from the candy store.

There was an old man who would snatch me from the
52 bus and mom didn't see.

Her head was turned, looking out the opposite window, while I disappeared inside the store of my foe.

He laughed. He said he'd get me. I ran and hid behind a chair so he wouldn't see me.

I remember breathing heavily and shaking nervously.

I could hear him breathing but voiceless was my screaming.

I pulled my legs in, Tightening, Shaking, Oh, So Frightening.

Huddled Behind the Chair ** then … I woke.

It was very upsetting many times each night, year after year. It didn't seem right.

This nightmare's recurring and haunting me, since Ms. Principal's touching was a trigger for me.

My subconscious self was telling me that it wanted to expel this malady.

Now, presently it is away from me. I worked it out. I am free.

THE COAL BIN

As a Child I had a second nightmare.
It was staged in my own basement.
I'd run and run around the furnace "island."
He, an old man, would chase me.
I was so scared.
When I thought I had gained some time,
I would bury myself in the coals in the coal bin.
He would enter the bin.
He'd say cackling,
"I know you're in here.
You can't get away now."
I would tremble.
He would start to poke at the coals
using the long pitchfork.
I could hardly catch my breath.
Then I would wake.

Confusion

My recurring nightmares frightened me.
I didn't know why it came several times each night.
I remember telling mom he was touching me,
But she told me it was alright.

The nightmares; playing again and again,
I was always running away
Or trying desperately to hide.
I remember breathing heavily.
Why are men chasing me?
Why am I running from them?
I hate men, I thought.
Why am I so alone?
Why is there not anyone here to help me?

Mommy said it was alright.

Playing horsie was lots of fun.
I liked riding on daddy's back.
We went around and around the table.
He would stop and roll me to the floor.
He would tickle and tickle.
I laughed and laughed
So hard that I cried.
And he wouldn't stop.
I'd cry so hard I would gasp for breath.
And he wouldn't stop.
He would lift my dress
And raspberry kiss my tummy and chest
And sometimes even below my panties.
Mom peaked in asking,
"What's going on?"
"Nothing," he said, as he threw his shoe.
She disappeared to somewhere.

Father liked it to be quiet.
If I made noise, as any child would,
He would stand up from his chair,
Unbuckle his belt,

Whip it out of his pants,
And hit me with it.
I would scurry and hide behind the chair.
I sat there for long times.
I learned to draw pictures
In the nap of the velvet cloth.
I didn't like him hitting me.
I would have red marks on my legs.
They loved to pull my long curly hair.
They didn't care if it hurt.

She told me not to tell
That my monthly visitor from age 10
Was a secret only ladies kept.
But he came in and sat on the bed,
Looked at me,
He laughed.
He said, "If you think you are in pain now girlie
Just wait until you have a baby."
I didn't know what he meant by that.
She betrayed me.
She told him.

I didn't like the yummy sounds
Coming from uncle tom.
He, too, would pull me close to him,
His hands clenching my upper arms.
For a "hug"
He would rub my chest up close against his body
And make noises.
It didn't feel good.
I wasn't allowed not to give him a "hug."
They made me.

She told me,
"You killed Grandpa!
You hurt your leg.
He worried about you.
He had a heart attack
And died."
She pointed her finger

At me while I was coloring
While lying on the living room floor.
I killed him.
I was bad.

No one wanted me
But everyone wanted to touch me.
I was confused.
I feared people.
I didn't know what they would do to me.
I felt alone.
I was a liar.
I was stupid.
She left me alone with him.
After sneaking out while I was in another room.
I'd cry for her.
I cried so hard that I couldn't catch my breath.
When I did cry father told me,
"If you cry I will give you
something to cry about.."
His eyes bulged out when he said that.
It was ugly
And frightening for me.

I learned to hate.
I learned not to tell.
I learned I must keep it inside.
I didn't cry for 33 years.
I was asked my opinion
And then told,
"No, that's not right."

Everyone did what they wanted to me.
No one stood up for me.
I felt lonely all the time.
I would dream a lot in my head.
I was always the best.
I could save the world.
It was good.
I was good.

I loved being in my fantasy world.
It was mine alone.
I owned it
And I could allow anyone I wanted
To come into it
Even if they were not real.
It was where I was accepted
As I was.

Then while I slept
Another night terror.
I could feel his ****
Rub up against me.
I would try to scream,

I couldn't,
It just wouldn't come out.
I struggled so hard.
I pushed and pushed.
I, at last, let out a tiny scream.
He stopped what he was doing,
Got up, and ran.
He didn't want to be caught.
I woke sweating, shaking.
My husband comforted me.

Most of the time was like this.
I was a loser
nobody wanted
or
everybody wanted.

MOMMY, WHERE ARE YOU?

You have always been my mother,
That I can't deny.
But where were you, Mommy,
When he'd make me cry?
Then when I did tell you
It was treated like a lie!

You didn't see him belt me,
Or pull my curly hair,
Or see my small frame slipping
Between the wall and chair,
Nor hear the slurs he'd call me
And the facial slaps I couldn't bear.
Nor see the glass of cold water
Thrown upon my back so bare.

He taught me well to hate him
And scurry, afraid to die.
Your neglect to see a problem
Denied me to feel or cry.

I understand that he was sick,
An untreated alcoholic he be.
I understand how you might have felt,
Having no supportive place to flee.

Still memories of years gone past
Are negative to me.
My wish that he be dead became
Suicidal ones you see.

So, where was my mommy?
Surely not near me.

You were in a situation not recognized back then.
Will history repeat itself? No, not to my kin.
You yourself have had those problems you deny to see,
For no protection from uncle nate –
Neither did you give to me.

Then when the witch she touched me all that I could see
Were the days that uncle nate surely had molested me.
My fear for any child going to that school,
Possibly being abused was against my rule.

It's a really, really sad thing
That you play a game called shame,
I didn't do anything – but live my life so lame.
I never would have known you see,
If it weren't for my friends.
The support that they have given me
Has helped me to mend.

So, again I ask, "Where were you?
And where you may be now?"
Me, I'm still surviving and I know I haven't lied.
But, I wish I'd had a mommy, for within me I had died.

You still choose not to "see" me now,
For shame I bring to you.
Your admittance and concern,
will be "knew" to view.

Understand… to live a healthy life
One must be guided, hugged, and praised,
Each special uniqueness is nurtured;
Confidence leads the way.

Yet in my darkest moments when all I wanted was to die,
Feeling so heavy a burden – You didn't even try?

How I truly want a mommy,
For her support I'd give a cheer.

It must be nice to have a mommy …

Someday …
        Sometime …
                Somewhere …

Things have seemed to be going ok. Every weekend we manage to find special time for the YMCA. I love to swim and so does my daughter. However, I feel anxious there. As helpful as the Y is for us, I'm surprised to find this being the home of the confrontations!

After a great swim, I was using the ladies room. All of a sudden, I wasn't alone. The younger Me was standing perpendicular directly in front of me. A man's hand was holding her shoulder. I looked - it was - him - uncle nate - right there in front of me - facing the younger me. I gasped. It was so clear I have never experienced a more real flashback. Then I was inside the child, she was scared. His round face donned with eyeglasses was so alive. He was there. She was terrified. She wanted to cry, but couldn't. She never looked at me. Back inside me I tried to reach her to pull her away. As close as they were to me, they were out of my reach. I thought - oh G-d, what does this mean?! I went back inside the child to help her pull away, but she was frozen to him. It was no use. I was frantic. I couldn't help her. Back to myself, looking at them posed together, I could feel her fright, her helplessness. They began to fade from their lucid realityness. Now, this flashback is a constant memory for me. I feel that terror, that helplessness. I, too, want to cry, but can't. I feel numb and so hurt, useless, and disappointed.

It is true. She was a child. She did nothing wrong. She couldn't help herself. I, the child, couldn't help me. I, the adult, still could not change what happened. I could not reach her. I tried so hard to reach her...

Where are You?

I am here, but she is over there quietly sitting in the grass, gently rubbing her hand over the deep green blades beside her. She looks so sad and so puzzled. She doesn't know who she is or why she was even born. She lives in a world she remembers little about. She enjoys; puppies, bunnies, butterflies, flowers, rainbows, lightning bugs, and especially, beaches. She is a gentle child. She cannot speak nor feel. She has no one to protect her since no one has in her past. At times she smiles and seems to be happy. I try to look into her face, but she won't allow it. She is alive within me; but like a seed that hasn't been natured, she hasn't been nurtured enough to grow in freedom. She is quite frightened and senses I am aware of her presence. I love her, but I am afraid she won't love me back. She has always been alone, but is conditioned to the circumstances and accepts them. My awareness of her has now become a threat to her being. Time continues to pass. I feel her presence in the back of my throat and in the burning tears in my eyes. How can I make her feel loved? How can I hug her? She is terrified of being hurt again. She trusts no one. I don't want her to run away. I want us to live together in peace. The pain of her being afraid of me lies deep and is real. Maybe if I can protect us she will trust me enough to share love. We will become friends and begin to enjoy the rest of our life. We can start by holding hands while walking barefoot as those gentle waves massage our feet. We will laugh, sharing all of what life offers. Using time we will be brave and strong as one to love our being.

Inner Child and Me

Occasionally, we all are that lost, scared, lonely little girl. She has no direction to go, no one to trust. That little girl needs to be nurtured and loved as she should have been long ago. We have to embrace her. We have to prove to her that no one is going to hurt her again. We have to stress to her that what happened was not her fault. My inner child is young. She doesn't remember much of her life at all.

There are times when she feels safe with what we are experiencing. You know, the good stuff. Yet, she is missing something. Bring her to the park. Ride the swings. It's fun. You can hear her giggle and see her smile, a smile that also ran from her life at a very young age. A smile that was turned upside down as her life did. Hug yourself as you will be hugging her.

She is so much a part of you. She may be more than one of you. She is there. To heal it is necessary to bring the two of you together.

Many times my fears are actually what she is feeling. Can she be holding me back from living? Surely she can. She is invisible to others. Take a moment to envision you holding her hand or sharing a book. She missed a lot of that. She has so much of life to catch up with. It won't be as it was then. It is today. She will be reborn today.

Enjoy your inner child! Enjoy the today!

Who's that Face?

Who's that face in the mirror?
A child it seems to be.
With curly locks and rosy cheeks
She does resemble me.

Who's that face in the mirror?
I haven't seen her in years.
She hardly cracks a smile,
She passes so many tears.

Who's that face in the mirror?
She certainly is pretty.
She's full of hatred for herself,
Oh, dear, what a pity.

Who's that face in the mirror?
A child all alone.
Passing each day in a lonely way,
A star that's never shone.

Who's that face in the mirror?
She lives in constant fear.
She rarely speaks to anyone,
Listening for who is near.

Who's that face in the mirror?
She seems on the alert.
She constantly is watching
So she no more will hurt.

Who's that face in the mirror?
This face is very still.
She stares out of the mirror,
To live, she has no will.

Who's that face in the mirror?
The child I'd call mine.
I'd give her love and lots of hugs,
All happiness so fine.

Who's that face in the mirror?
I struggle through each day.
My inner child did survive,
Now she's here to stay.

Behind the Chair

You saw me,
You wanted me,
You had me.
Now, the child inside sees you,
Wants to hurt you,
While the adult outside
Does not do it.
She wants to cut you
So that you hurt.
She wants to cut it off forever.
She wants you maimed
The way her life was discarded.
Now, she wants it now
For it is too late to make up for those hellish years
And the days of today
And all the tomorrows.
She wants you punished for something you did
And for the nothing she received from you in return.
You fuckin' bastard.
Die in hell. You deserve it.
Your evil eyes and thoughts and deeds
Will have the pain you have given me all the days of my life
From that day and for everyday that followed.
Your delight will now be the pain of all of us children
As you now hold your member in the palms of your hands
Holding it up to G-d.
In all the pain and anguish and devastation,
I want you dead you bastard …
The life of the living dead for all you bastards …
Just like all of our children inside.
But, for you it is different
For you deserve the pain.

Your prized possession,
Your trophy,
Now feels the pain.
Your head feels the pain.
You and satan forever.
My child is still prisoner of your delight in war,

This on going war.
May your most valuable member be discarded
As the lives you discard.
And of the moms who discard.
And round it spins.
The desire,
The deed,
The delight,
Bring to death the child
Who never played,
Who never understood her feelings,
Who fears the world,
Who wonders what next.
She is alive hiding inside
For there are lots of you,
And lots of unbelievers,
And lots of deniers.
My wish to G-d
For you is suffering in hell
For all of your days …
That is my gift.
That gift to you cannot compare
To my gift from you.
I don't like presents.
I don't like pasts.
I fear futures,
And I fear every him I see.
I fear the child's fears
And her adult home does not feel safe.
Her adult cannot forget the horror feelings
You gave her child.

She still hides behind the chair.
It is safe there for a while,
For as long as today needs it to be.
The child is a vital part of her life.
She can trust the chair will not hurt her.
The chair gave her
The opportunity to withdraw into nap art …

The kitchen now finds her safety from the bell.

The kitchen provides the tools I need to maim you
As you have maimed me.
The kitchen owns the knife
As you own your thoughts and deeds.
To maim you as you have maimed me …
For you still receive less than you gave me.
My want will never be truth as your want was received.
My want,
Through my tears,
Is to maim you …
All of you out there.
My child wants to do that …
Her adult is trapped.
Her desires to maim all of you are behind her adult wall.
You cannot see her,
But she is there
In her anger,
And her pain.
She is there.
She lives heavily with pain.
She lives each day despairingly.
She breathes
Until one day her adult will die,
But she will live forever in pain.
She meets G-d.
Forever she begs G-d not to forgive you.
You are satan's brother,
You are all his family.

You are the evil of the world.
You are the terrorist.
You want it all at anyone's expense.
G-d, stop the evil.
Turn the world over to live …
Without evil,
Live in the peace meant to be lived.
Live in the hope of Heaven.
Live in the peace, in happiness, and well-being
So that my next child will be free
To enjoy the pleasures of life you give.
Live, child, live …

My child, the future is yours to live.

I see you male
With your possession,
With your wants, desires, and deeds.
I see you male.
I will never forget.
Would we be mentally ill
Had we not been abused
And used, abused, used, abused …
What would I be now?
What would she be?
Was/Is this her fate – to bring abuse issues
Into the open for all to see?
I am a descendant of innocence.
He is a descendant of evil.
Can I stop evil?
Can I?

I am one little girl in an adult disguise.
Maybe with her help we can …

Some More

I didn't like being tickled
And tickled some more
And some more.

I didn't like to hear his sound
And smell his breath
Some more.

I didn't like to smell the odor,
Odor from under his arms,
Some more.

I hated to feel his sandpapered face
On my neck, on my tummy, under my panties,
Some more.

I didn't like the tickle game, nope.
You know it'd make me cry and sob …
Some more and more.

Not Fair

Oh, It's morning …
I don't want to go to School –
The walk is long and sometimes lonely –
I look down as I walk –
I think about mom –
I worry about her –
I am afraid that he might hurt her again –
I am at school –
I should be concentrating –
I am thinking about mom –
I am not listening to the teacher –
It is lunchtime –
I sit alone at the one–sided table –
I face the wall –
I eat my tomato sandwich ma made me –
I think about her –
I hope she is safe –
I like to keep her safe –
I always worry about her –
I am always afraid he would hurt her –
He yells, he throws things, he hits us –
He makes her cry –
He touches me –
He tickles me to tears –
He hits me with his belt –
I hide behind the chair –
He wet kisses me –
He rubs his stubbles on me –
His whiskers are scratchy –
I can smell his cologne, body,
        cigarettes, alcohol –
It is hard feeling safe in my family –
I never felt special or important –
I learned to "jump" when he'd call me
        "sweetie?" –
He throws ice water on our backs
        during a bath –
He called me a "fuckin' whore" and
        "sonofabitch" –

I learned to avoid him as much as
        possible –
I think about dying a lot –
I didn't know this was not natural –
Fix it, do it over, it's not fair –

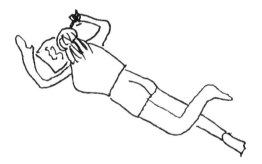

Pre — Suicidal

Wondering quite a bit, at times I don't know who I am anymore or even who I was – whether or not that was really me or what was to have been me – if this makes any sense at all. I know where I came from – I think. Where I am going is quite a mystery or why am I going at all. Sometimes all I want to do is cry, but it never happens. I don't cry nor do I show this side of me to anyone. This has always been "private." I don't like to hurt anyone yet just take "hurt" for granted. It is easier to suppress and continue – accept and go on up to now, but for how much longer. The denial is ripping me apart. How could a person do such a thing? Life's values mean nothing. My normally tolerant, cheerful personality has become one of devastation. My mask is blown. My body feels hollow. The grief is overwhelming. The goals I once had mean nothing. I have no strength nor desire to think about them. I cannot imagine my life free from this. I feel like a marionette or a robot … doing because someone else demands it. It's just routine. I have made designated "safe" places and "high risk" places. I would like to be away – forever. Nothing matters anymore – the summer, the pool, the beach – they will always be there for someone else to love as much as I have loved them. They do nothing for me as they once refilled my outlook with a smile. I can't relax enough to enjoy them anymore for these other events are constantly on my mind. They don't go away. I'm not sure if they ever will – it's part of me forever. I cannot live peacefully with a denial. The pain is intense — unlike anything I have ever experienced in my life up to this point. I do not comprehend how it could get better. I cannot speak to anyone nor should I even try. I fear their negative opinions. I am not strong. Help me to make sense of it all. Help me to stop spinning, to ease the pain. Be there for me, be concerned, for I don't know how much I can take – alone. I am tired. My love now is sleep – for only then I am free.

FEELING BAD

Have thought about calling Therapist when feeling so bad and wanting to swallow my pills —die. I was able to go to a meeting earlier, but couldn't continue the charade. I asked her how many pills will it take, how many? I wonder why DID I Call Her? I couldn't have been dead then. I wasn't finished. My child needed school items and I needed to be sure the beast wouldn't be near her. My sons were older, but still needed a mom. I couldn't abandon them the way I was abandoned. It hurt then and it hurts now. I'm an "orphan" in my own right. Why they didn't want me then I don't know. Why they ran away from me, I don't know. I am saddened by it. It would have been nice to have had family support. Biological support is what I have none of. When I think about being with them I fear their behaviors. Will I continue to be belittled and considered invaluable? I don't need that. I don't miss my biological family. I wish I'd been born to a different family who would have been supportive of each other I wonder what it is about me to make them treat me as though I'm poison. Yes, they have issues. I understand. I was chosen to be the "black sheep". Oh, well. I'm in a better place now. I don't want to regress.

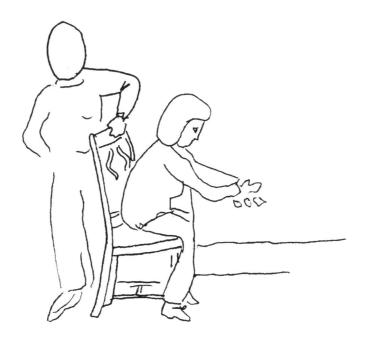

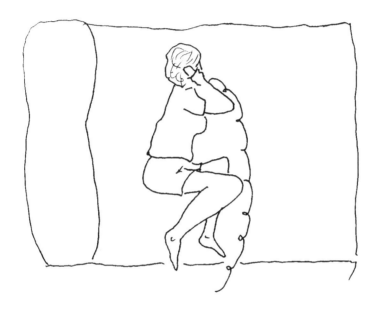

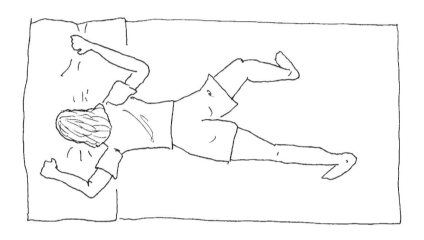

You Turned Me Away …

You turned me away …
You laughed at the way my toes point outward when I walk.
You ridiculed the way I cooked and cleaned.
You hated my husband and his family though, when you wanted to be, you were his best friend.
You spent holidays with others – not me, not my family.
You used me as your chauffer … I thought I was being obedient.
You chose my clothes.
You allowed relatives to speak down to me.
You would ask for my opinion and then immediately disagree with it.
You called me a "slob" as your mother did to you.

You pushed me away with all your negativity.

You didn't believe me when I told you about uncle nate.
You blamed me for killing Grandpa.
You laughed at me.
You never defended me.
You said, "Shame on You" to me a lot.

You pushed me away.

You refused to recognize he belted me.
You wanted to rule other people … or just me.
You said, "I used to be able to control you, now I can't anymore."
You kicked me, hit me, and knocked my chair up on two legs as I sat on it.
You said, "Don't call me to dinner, I mean it," so I didn't.
You didn't tell them that.

You pushed me away … far away … out of reach.

You verbally attacked me when you thought no one else was near … and got caught one day.

You pushed me a little at a time for years and years.

You belittled my friends.
You belittled me in front of my friends.

You pushed my friends away.
You didn't like my children's friends.
You allowed your son to call names to my daughter's friend.
You spent time with people who misused alcohol – including yourself.
You allowed dad to abuse us.
You refused to validate that.
You tried to change my ways to conform with others who had changed yours.

You pushed me away.

You let them laugh at my large breasts.
They all laughed at me.
You yelled at me for running away.   I ruin everything.
You always blamed me.
You told me I was "dirty" during menstruation and I couldn't shower.
You told me if I touched a flower during this same time that it would die.

You didn't explain the police in the living room after finding a dead, almost naked, lady in the brook behind our house … "Come Softly to Me" played on the radio.

You didn't explain why our teenaged neighbor was stabbed to death at the summer lake home, his dog later passed away, and his grieving mother wailed for years day and night.

You didn't explain why your employee and his friend committed suicide inside a car.
You kept it secret about my cousin's dad kidnapping him.

You tried to cling to your mother but she clung to someone else.
You let her cling to you when she was sick.
You let her come into our home whenever she desired.
She was found rummaging through the closet.
I threw a sugar bowl at her. I was wrong. That isn't ok.

You pushed me away.

You told me I was sick.
You told me I was crazy.
You told me, "You need help."
You allowed me to be mistreated by your son and his family.

You pushed me away.

You weren't there when he belted my legs and I hid behind the tapestry chair in fear of him.
You didn't see him slap me across my face as my friend did. She ran home.
You didn't explain why he slept outside on the porch.
Your actions didn't give me happy memories.
You said, "What's mine is mine and what's yours is mine."
You clearly stated what was yours constantly.
You were in charge of my puppetting.

You made me kiss and hug people to show "respect" while they showed none as they rubbed their chest back and forth across mine.
You let him throw cold water on my back while bathing, then he'd laugh, "ha, ha." I was a teenager. How humiliating.

You pushed me away.

You cared more for your cousins than for me when being told again about my being molested by uncle nate, their father.

You pushed me away.

You neglected me at this most critical time in 1993.
You abandoned me.

You minimized my pain by telling me, "People have been raped and do better than you ..." Maybe other people had her mother by her side. You told me, "She can't believe what you say is true," minimizing again.

You just kept pushing me away.

You had your chance. I thought you would take it.
You disappointed me.

You denied me of unconditional love.
You contributed to my lost life.

You were highly successful at pushing me away.
      I hope you are proud.

Disappointments, Judgments, Validation

Although all of this was happening I was relieved. I truly felt that this was the cause of my madness and I knew this would bring my family together.

It did not. It did the opposite.

Bro wished that I would be feeling better psychologically and emotionally and a few moments later said I was resentful and jealous over mother's happiness. Hhmmm ... That happiness was for her to be with her boyfriend and her granddaughter, his daughter.

My pain was for my four children. They were never denied a grandmother.

My husband and I were disrespectful, psychologically abusive, and lived in a dysfunctional atmosphere. It was of these ... He and I were slaves to brother and mother. When they spoke we responded even to the point of driving mother to his home to sit his daughter. What a shock it was for them to hear the word, "No," and for us to stick by it. Disrespectful? Dysfunctional? Abusive? Hhmmm ...

Obsessed and absorbed in my past rather than being concerned about caring for others, not have them come to you is what I next heard. Hhmmm ... My past was just suddenly thrust into my eyes. It would have been psychologically beneficial to have had my family support me.

Only one aunt asked me what this was all about. When I told her she ran straight to mother. I could hear her say, "Why didn't you believe her? You know he had that reputation." Silence followed. I was validated. Good! No, not good.

I was told by brother there is still great opportunity to redeem my life. I have time to become a loving, caring mother to my children who lived with anger, lack of affection, and insanity.

Also, to become a loving, respectful daughter to an unperfect mother. Well, no one is perfect. We each do what we can with the resources at hand or can make available to us. Support is most important especially when it comes from immediate family.

I have one judge. I now have peace, harmony, and self-respect as do my husband and my children.

I was told that I must have done something right as all of my children turned out just fine. Hhmmm ... They are each of great sense of self, well-respected, gracious adults all of whom have excellent careers and lovely families. They each have a uniqueness about them that when they enter a room each is immediately noticed in a positive manner.

Yes, I worked long, hard, tough years to up-grade my family. To change is a challenge and I took that challenge and am successful.

It shows. It feels great! We are victorious!
They, the dysfunctional, are stuck in the past.

I'm Confused

At the time I realized that there was a reason for my "madness." I thought it would bring the family closer together. I was wrong. I was left alone, once again, in believing the issue was my fault. I was abandoned. I would have felt very highly of you if you had stayed to support me. I saw more "power" in your doing that. Rather than be strong to face the issue, you flew away. Now, you want me back? I'm confused.

How do I unlock the frozen heart? Freezing my heart was a survival method I had chosen rather than be overcome by the past leading to self-checkout.

What is Love?

What is love anyway?
And where does it come from? … hm?
Is it something we are born with
Like a head with two eyes?
Is it something that is learned
From others in our lives?
Can we touch it? Can we feel it?
Do we keep it tucked inside …
Until …
We want to use it for something,
Or someone,
Or wear it firm with pride? … hm?
Is it shared by those who guide us
Through this journey we call life?
Is it thick? Is it thin?
Can you spread it with a knife?
Does it look for me? Or want me?
Does it come to me in silence
Like a dainty butterfly?
Does it sound like crackling wood
Of a warm fireside?
Does it jingle like the sleigh-bells
On horses in the park?
Does it slip inside my body
In the night when it is dark?
Does it let me know it's with me
Like the thunder of the storm?
Does it stay a little while
Or is eternity the norm? … hm?
Will I truly ever know …
If it dies within me, or will forever grow?
Help me find what love is …
Tell me where to look.
Do I buy it in the store? …
Or learn it from a book?
Let me know what love is …
Don't I have the right to know
How to own it, how to share it,
How to hold it, how to feel it? …

Let me know what love is,
How expensive is its cost?
Help me find where love is,
Mine is surely lost.

WHAT DO I THINK OF ME?

SOMETHING HAPPENED

Something Happened
My body is trying to tell me.
It was a long time ago.
Long before I could remember.

Something Happened
I can feel the piercing pain.
It must have been that way.
It jabs so sharp and quick
That it takes my breath away.

This piercing, breathtaking vaginal pain
Feels like something
Being pushed there.
My body is telling me
Someone raped me.

Someone raped me …
Someone raped me of my innocence.
Someone raped me of my childhood.
Someone raped me of my life.

Someone …

Who is that someone?

WHO AM I?

Who am I?

I do not know.
It all began
Some time ago.

What is my purpose?
What is my call?
Sometimes I feel
I face a brick wall.

I have talents,
So they say.
All developed
The wrong way.

I'm very timid,
Very shy.
For 33 years
I didn't cry.

My huge, ugly body
Was always quite numb.
My emotions I feared
Would never come.

Anger, Rage, Intimidation,
What a terrible strife.
Laughing, hugging, singing,
A child asked of life.

You shouldn't, you can't,
Was what I heard.
Sonofabitch, fuckin' whore,
Am I of these words?

He fondled my breasts.
She said he loves me.
He wet kissed my lips

And nibbled my body.

I never knew
What was to be.

While in high school
I passed a test,
A letter from the Pentagon
Looking for the best.

However, my fears
And anxieties
Kept me where
I "want to be?"

How could I survive?
I cannot trust,
Easily startled …
Can't is a must.

So, I thought about dying
And do to this day.
Suicide – close,
But not today.

Who am I?
I struggle.
Changes … more changes.
Oh, how I juggle.

Who am I?
I wonder what should
Be my potential?
Can it be good?
With self-esteem
So very low,
Lost confidence,
Does it show?

I stutter and shake
And fear oh so much.

Co-dependent,
Making decisions,
Living robotic,
Way out of touch.

Who am I?
I wonder.
Bringing bad things your way.
Who am I?
I struggle
With this everyday.

Paralyzed by Fear

He is there …
        Watching, waiting.

I can't see him.
I don't know where he is.
But I can feel him.

Lurking, waiting, just for me.

He follows me.
My heart races.
Where can I go?
Where can I hide?
He feels closer.
I look around.
I sense him.
I can feel his stare on me.
I can feel his breath.
My body is quivering.
My heart is pounding.

Where can I go?

Just here, nowhere,
As he is always

Lurking, waiting …

        Just for me …

Defeated

As I sit here all alone, I wonder …

Of what I was to be, if I had been born differently,

Or what I'd think of me, had this not been my reality,

Of a rising self so straight and tall, "dream" side of me; I'm meek 'n' small,

Of my always changing mood, from being solemn then to lewd,

If when I am being "raging mad," I would not if the choice I had,

Of loving and hating and tired of waiting, to not feel bad,

Of life the way it should have been,

I feel as though I never win.

Wrong Way Love

Feelings about love surround me now. I don't know love the way others do. I can't use the word when I don't have the feeling … yet, what is the feeling?

I have feelings of being inadequate. A mother's love and acceptance – unconditionally – is very important. I understand the behaviors of both parents, but WHY was it me they chose to be their target for all of their inadequacies … for their dysfunctional behavior … for the placement of their history. Why was it me? Why didn't she love me enough to protect me from all of them? Why didn't she let her love for me – if it was there – be felt by me. I was always alone. I felt like an outcast. I wished I could have been adopted. That would feel special … He was extremely violent; she was extremely meek. Why did they have me? Why was I born? My life should never have been.

I am afraid to love. I feel embarrassed by my feelings or actions. In my head I'd like to make love in different ways. In reality I'm really quite coy regarding this subject. I am so confused. My feelings are messed up. I don't have sexual feeling. I don't feel arousal. What is it I'm supposed to feel – I have no clue?

Love was the portrait of pain and violence. It was hitting and hurting and slapping. It was a lack of tears. It was turning inward with pain and embarrassment and shame. It was wet kisses and stubble rubbing. It was being called a bitch and a sweetie within minutes. It was intense fear and hatred. How do I love? Define Love? I can't.

I wanted the love I knew. To get it I tormented my husband intensely. I called him a "Wimp" because he wouldn't hit me. I edged him on to the point when he finally did slap my face. Then he asked, "Are you happy?" as he left the house.

What affects will this have on me? More importantly, what affects will this have on my children? They deserve better. They deserve more than I know how to give. How will this behavior affect their lives? I should have never had children, but I did. I did because I wanted someone to love me. With my past rages there must have been times when they must have hated me. Is it too late?

WHO? ME?

I was lonely growing up.
Once I had several girlfriends
And one boyfriend.
I talked to others sometimes.
But my "love" and "life" was a dream,
Nothing but a fantasy.
I wanted more but I was afraid.
I didn't even know who I could ask.
I was alone within my head.
I am really "neat" in my head.
I am the winner, the best.
I am pretty, petite, and thin.
What a fantasy!
I can save anyone
If they're female and being abused.
How strange? I didn't know it then.
I also adopted lots of children
To keep them safe … all girls.
That is all inside my head.
Then one day, not so long ago
Into my ears came,
"You were snobbish and stuck-up,
That's why we didn't talk to you,
That's what we thought".
I didn't talk because I was afraid.
My social skills are poor still.
I've missed out on a lot of living.
My "good ole" days were days of fear.
They passed. I can't get them back.

God, Why Did You Do This?

I don't understand You, G-d,
Creator of All Things.
Why is there evil?
I am confused, G-d,
You are "All Forgiving."
How can You forgive
A child abuser?
Must I prove my endurance,
My worthiness to You, G-d?
I am tired, G-d,
Tired of this path.
Where is my unconditional love?
Where is my innocence?
You made them evil
And they took them from me.
How can I believe You, G-d?
How can I trust my religion?
G-d, do you even know
Which religion is Your religion?
Faith and Hope cannot exist.
Why? Where do I go from here?
Did you see me G-d?
Couldn't You stop them G-d?
Do You hear me now?

Livin'?

Livin' my life
And never feeling loved
Not even by Mother …

I felt alone,
I was afraid.
I thought I was like all others.

I love my children
But that is different
Than the love you receive from a mother.

And the one who loves me
I can't say it from me,
He says, "I Love You!" like no other.

The "love" part of me
Confused, blocked steadfastly,
I know not if I should bother.

I can't understand
Why someone would love
Someone not loved by her mother.

New Perspective

There are things in life you know
The good, the bad,
The opposite,
The happy and the sad.
The highs, the lows,
The upside downs,
You know how it goes.

Why do we judge one another?

When we hear our intuition
But somehow do not listen,
To the words we are receiving,
We falter.

The time to understand oneself
Is the greatest gift to me,
A brand-new light, a new perspective,
I understand what came to be.

Yet, a "twist" lives deep within me
I cannot understand,
When down and out as I was,
Did she not extend her hand?

Out of My Hands

"Tis time to speak with courage and pride,
What I've been feeling deep inside.

It's been too long for me to wait,
It's more than I can tolerate.

Harassment, ridicule and shame,
Were added by you next to my name.

I've wished and waited for you to love me,
But now I know it's naught to be.

What happened prior to "93,
Was more painful than you desire to see …

However, all the days since then
Were most vital in helping me mend.

I needed support and love from you,
But that's not what you chose to do.

A "child" I am at forty-five,
You hit me still and minimize.

"Forget it," you said. "People have worse."
"You're brainwashed," you added to the curse.

Maybe brainwashed, yes you see,
Washed out of inept indignities.

A new, amazing, important, confident me …
Metamorphosis, as a butterfly, I will be free.

I'm closing the door on this chapter of time.
I shall be no longer blind.

Influenced by your body language
And your words of hate,

I have decided for your acceptance,
I can no longer wait.

So, you go your way and I'll go mine.
I wonder if peace you'll one day find.

As I breathe, life passes me by ...

I am rumbled, for now I feel feelings of being abandoned,
lied to, hated, angered, terribly saddened and it is oh so painful –

I breathe as I watch from my eyes the world around me, it frightens me, I am
so frozen; it is awful –

I breathe as I see my history click on the screens of my mind; it never goes
away; how pitiful –

I breathe as I peer out my window, I think of the hustle and bustle of people
scurrying about and of me in all my sadness and loneliness; how sorrowful –

I breathe as I feel so ashamed of myself, for not being all I could be, for not
reaching my potential; how disgraceful –

I breathe as I wonder why my life was, why it has been as it is, and worry where
it will go, why, and when, how, my time; how wasteful –

I breathe as I spin within my own "special" world, doing nothing, nor nothing
alone; how distressful –

I breathe and I weep for me, for all my losses and sorrows and pain, with all
my inequities, with my lack of self and self-worth, they patrol my being; how
powerful –

I breathe as I am with my isolated self; fear rules me, I abhor me, wish to
annihilate me; how unlawful –

I breathe as I dream of a future, as I yearn to banish this pain of many years,
to go home to G-d before being whole; my cries I muffle –

As I breathe I wonder if this butterfly will ever be free, I wonder what it would
be to really be me without such history; quite incomprehensible –

As I breathe, life passes me bye ...

She Failed You

I couldn't concentrate in school.
      She Failed Me.
I feared going to Brownies or to the concert.
      She failed Me.
I wanted to feel pretty.
      She failed Me.
I wanted to have friends, both girls and guys.
      She failed Me.
I wanted to be loved.
      She failed Me.
I wanted to be free to dance, sing, and laugh.
      She failed Me.
I wanted to be famous, to do bigger, better things.
      She failed Me.
I saw my past in front of me as she touched me.
      She failed Me.
I felt the pain of the past now unprotected.
      She failed Me.
I am now exposed … everyone knows.
      She failed Me.
I grew wiser becoming too much for her.
      She failed Me.
I became very ill with intense pain.
      She failed Me.
I was hospitalized, in therapy, and taking medication.
      She failed Me.
I would be startled if someone came up behind me.
      She failed Me.
I held my body tense. My ears never slept. My eyes
            Always open.
      She failed Me.
I kept my emotions inside. I hadn't cried in 33 years.
      She failed Me.
I stutter, shrink, and hide.
      She failed Me.
I tried to stop feeling suffocated by using nasal spray.
      She failed Me.
I was confused about love.
      She failed Me.

I could smell, hear, and feel him.
> She failed Me.

I felt validated and safe.
> She failed Me.

I grew in leaps and strides how to help me.
> She failed Me.

I learned to feel my pain and cried with her.
> She failed Me.

I learned to take care of me by going to the doctors.
> She failed Me.

I learned it is ok to be good to me.
> She failed Me.

I learned I was loving and valuable.
> She failed Me.

I learned that by working with children I was
> comforting me.
> She failed Me.

I learned we were separate beings inside of one.
> She failed Me.

I believed she would never leave me as she promised
> She wouldn't.
> She failed Me.

I, too, felt the magnetism between us. She called it
> Adopted Family.

I sometimes hear his words of the past as were so
> Clearly spoken that day.

Now I hear …
> She Failed You.

Your Loss, Not Mine

It finally occurred to me,
'Twas such a waste of time.
I feel a sense of value now,
Much more than a dime.

My character is one to you
Of tattered grit and grime.
You spread ourselves so far apart ~
Truth is ~ Your Loss, Not Mine.

No One Cries for Me

No one knows the pain I'm in,
No one knows the agony
Of each and every day …
To rise from bed,
To step foot to the floor,
To drag to groom.

No one knows how hard it is
To dress daily,
To shower/shave,
To wash my hair.

No one knows how hard it is
To concentrate,
To complete just one task at a time,
To sit during one TV show.

No one knows how difficult it is
To walk outside my own home,
To bring in the mail,
To make telephone calls.

No one knows how I wonder
Why I'm chatting constantly
At a family gathering while at the same time
I am not knowing myself …
And while speaking, silently asking myself why?

No one knows the struggles
To just push off the shadows
That loom inside my head.

No one knows how sad I feel,
How guilty and ashamed.
No one knows of where I've been
Nor how my day be framed.

No one knows the heaviness all the gray days bring.
No one knows the energy only the sun can sing.

No one knows … No, no one knows,
No one cries for me.

Who was that?

My daughter and I had spent some time at the mall. On the way up the escalator almost to the top near the third floor, I saw a man behind me. He was small, wearing dark pants and a white shirt with rolled up sleeves … similar to father. He was so close I could feel him breathing on me. I had turned away and then back again at the top of the escalator. I stepped straight ahead. He stepped to the right. I watched him take three steps.

She asked, "What are you doing?"

I asked her if there was a man behind me on the escalator?

"No," she said.

I said, "Yes and he walked over there. But, I don't see him now."

"No one was there," she insisted.

"I saw him," I said.

She laughed saying, "You're funny."

* * * * *

This was the closest a "figure" has been to me. It is the first in a long time. I wondered if he could have been a ghost, his ghost? I had become anxious. My breathing was heavier when I felt his presence and could see him from the corner of my left eye as we approached the top of the escalator. He was standing on the very next step.

FOR ME?

I wonder when my life will end,
Who shall it be who will descend,
To come for me?

I wonder why this life won't end?
I've tried but seems I'll never mend,
So come for me.

I wonder why my life won't blend
With others, of purpose; so do send
Someone for me.

I wonder why this time you lend
To me, oh G-d, I've tried to tend
The sheep you've given me.

I have failed you right through this day,
There is nothing you can say,
A useless life for me.

A waste of time, can't be ignored
The history has been explored,
Never will it leave me.

I'm sad, I'm sorry it is this way,
I'd hoped that a brighter day
Would stay with me.

So, I wonder when I'll go –
I've got a job to do you know,
Strengthen me.

I need courage to carry on,
So the poison will be all gone
From deep within me.

I need support of family and mentor,

Still being discouraged from deep inner core

Remembering the me.

I will do better,
        I will promise …

I promise
        to THINK and

          To act and speak like this —

           Giving peace to me.

Do You Love Me?

Do You love me …
I've no clue…
I don't know…
If I love you…

I don't know
If I want to kiss,
Does it feel
Like someone's fist?

I don't know
If I want to touch.
Quite uncomfortable…
Oh, so much.

I don't think
I want to feel,
My body is numb,
It's not real.

I don't think
I can hug.
What I am used to
Is pull and tug.

Inside my mind
I cannot tell,
There's slobbers and stubbles
And whew! What a smell!

Then down on the floor
Being tickled to tears
Or slipping behind
The safety of chairs.

This body was meek,
This body was small,
Its ears never slept,
Nope, not at all.

Its life was a fantasy,
Dreams were the norm.
Always prepared
For the raging storm.

But why was it then
I'd never learned love?
Nor how to cry …
What are tears made of?

I'm learning. I think.
It's nice knowing how
To be patient, kind, gentle,
PRESENT — meaning NOW!

IMAGINE ...

Imagine what the world would be
If there were no one in it just like me.
Survivors trying to cope with their pain,
Question if ever the relief they will gain.
Silently holding the secret inside
Having no one in whom to confide.
Thought of often but rarely said
The abused and neglected are better off dead.
It causes anger and rage that can kill,
As is the base problem of many mentally ill.
Those inflicting this terrible crime
Be it done unto them, rather than time.
Dysfunctionalism in the world would drastically drop,
Abuse and neglect must finally stop.
Sensitivity and compassion would likely rise,
Confidence, trust, and pride would be wise.
Survivors turned thrivers would surely be,
If only MY LIFE could be given back to me.

LOSSES:

My Innocence
My Childhood
My Adolescence
My Adulthood
My Feeling –
        Physically, Emotionally, Sexually, Mentally
My Trusting
My Believing
My Happiness
My Laughter
My Singing
My Smile
My Inquisitiveness
My Freedom
My Truthfulness
My Career
My Independence
My Sense of Worthiness
My Pride
My Confidence
My Security
My Self-Esteem
My Religion
My Living
Myself …

Almost - My Life …

Living Under the Influence of Abuse

My abuser still has control over me ...

When I fear ...
         Strangers
         Leaving home alone
         Taking a shower while home alone
         Making telephone calls
         Receiving telephone calls
         Bringing in the mail
         The ringing of the doorbell

When I feel shame by being embarrassed ...
         With my body
         When I stutter
         When I forget

When I don't speak what is on my mind ...
When I don't think I am as good as others ...
When I don't believe people when they
         Compliment me...
When I don't take care of my health ...

Depression

This is the illness of all illnesses. It should be classified
as the supreme destroyer of life, the most serious and as devastating as an
earthquake or some other natural disaster.

There is no controlling the feelings that ripple through the mind and body
even on the simplest of days. It's an exhausting, hellish life – one you'd like
to "give up" to everyone or even no one.

The smallest things upset me.

I push to catch up to time.

I don't like me because I don't know who I am.

I have no confidence in me.

Many times my fuse is short.

I feel even though I am with people, I am separate –
spaced out … dissociate.

I don't know how much longer I'm to have strength to "hold on." Self-
checkout seems to be the answer.

I am disappointed in feeling exhausted after short periods of time.

I cannot be busy for two consecutive days.

I do wish to feel normal, whatever that is.

Stop the agony.

I Want

I want yesterday …
I want it to be fixed.
I want anything thrown to be bubbles.
I want the insults to be praise.
I want the shames to be smiles.
I want the hitting to be hugs.
I want the molesting to be unthinkable.
I want the abusing to be abolished.
And I'd like to hear, "I love you."
I'd like to be encouraged, not ridiculed.
I'd like not to be embarrassed,
Nor to stutter.
I'd like to be believed …
I'd like a new beginning.

I have today,
I have been working hard for all of my todays.
Lots has changed … I can try.
Lots will change … I will learn more about me.
I HATE change …
I fear change's affects on me …
I fear everything …
People, crowds, going alone, speaking – what to say,
What will they think of me?
Will I be criticized?
What would I think of me if I were someone else?
I fear living.
Yet, I must live to change my destiny …
Or is this my destiny?

Tomorrow? I want tomorrow.
I want to be in the warm sunlight
In a field of wildflowers and butterflies.
I want to be on the beach with
The sounds of the surf and the sea gulls …
I want the darkness with its evening voices singing
And the bright moon, planets, and stars
Flickering above.
And the falling star … I did see it fall to earth.

And sometimes I want the showers for their glorious
Rainbows … may that pot of gold be mine.
I want tomorrow; the freedom of tomorrow
When I will share peacefully my experiences with you …
So you won't feel so alone,
Then, we can get through today.

I Learned

What I learned while growing up
 I thought every child experienced.
 I learned they didn't.

I experienced harm from others.
 I built a wall.
 I learned to hide.

I experienced fear.
 I was afraid of people.
 I learned to use "radar."

I experienced betrayal.
 I kept information inside.
 I learned not to trust.

I experienced humility.
 I was embarrassed.
 I learned shame.

I experienced ridicule.
 I was laughed at.
 I learned I lost self-worth.

I experienced abandonment.
 I was lonely.
 I learned to be shy.

I experienced blame.
 I was at fault.
 I learned how to be guilty.

I experienced death.
 I was able to kill people.
 I learned I was a murderer.

I experienced criticism.
 I was always wrong.
 I learned I wasn't good enough.

I experienced anxiety.
        I heard myself stutter.
        I learned to keep quiet.

I experienced fantasizing.
        I learned I was safe, loved, and respected there.
        I learned to dissociate.

I experienced uncomfortable touch.
        I wasn't believed and kept feelings inside.
        I learned to be numb.

I experienced having to do everything for others.
        I was not appreciated for my efforts.
        I learned how it feels to be used.

I experienced sexual play with friends.
        I played this game without anyone's knowledge.
        I learned to keep secrets.

I experienced others telling me, "You're sick."
        I was an outcast.
        I learned not to take care of my health.

I experienced name calling and ridicule.
        I felt alone and denied growth.
        I learned I've no sense of self.

I experienced wet kisses and unsafe touch.
        I needed to be believed.
        I learned to deny my feelings.

I experienced being pushed aside.
        Nobody wanted me near them.
        I learned there was something wrong with me.

I experienced meeting expectations.
        I found others did not.
        I learned disappointment.

I experienced being stifled.
        I don't know my potential.
        I learned not to take risks.

I learned love meant pain.
        I still don't like me.
        I learned to hurt myself.

I witnessed him grabbing and shaking his genitals at me.
        I was confused.
        I learned distorted ideas regarding sexuality.

I witnessed anger being expressed by rage.
        I don't control anger.
        I learned it is ok to throw things.

I heard, "Be Brave."
        I wore a mask.
        I learned how to hide my feelings.

I learned unconditional love is not necessarily the rule.
        I did not learn the joy of love.
        I learned hatred.

I always wanted to be liked and loved.
        I tried hard to be loveable.
        I learned I was not-worthy.

I experienced loss.
        It is traumatically painful.
        I learned loss never leaves you.

I learned to feel pain and anguish.
        I was connected to my feelings and emotions.
        I learned how to cry.

I experienced agony.
        I suffer depression.
        I learned one must be nurtured to feel safe enough to grow.

I experienced childbirth and real love.

I know the love to my children is the ultimate.
I learned love now feels good.

I experienced formal religion.
    I find G-d in Butterflies and Nature.
    I learned to be holy one doesn't need to be
    surrounded by walls.

I sought help for myself through good friends.
    I learned how to care for myself.
    I learned I am capable.

I discarded negatives from my life.
    I am surrounded by those who appreciate me.
    I learned I can make myself happy.

I learned I, too, am human.
    I know humans aren't perfect.
    I learned I am perfect as I am.

I learned that I want to be remembered in this world.
    I have walked a secret path.
    I will let others know that they are not alone.
    I learned I can and will help others.

SUICIDE ...

The fastest way
          to be locked into all
of your problems ...

FOREVER!

Self-checkout isn't the answer. It
gives horrific pain and emotional and
mental issues in those you love, those
who love you. Don't throw this guilt
onto them.

Reach out.

Rise above it.

Dear Abuse …

You are there. Are you willing to hear me? You are always so ignorant. Come out of hiding.

Abuse, have you hurt a life yet today? Have you mistreated anyone or even your pet? Have you raged causing terror to those you "love?" How can you claim you love? You do the opposite and worse. You don't claim responsibility for your actions. You, yourself, "BIG BOSSY" monster while abusing … then you are yellow – chicken. Why??? Why are you "afraid" to tell the police you smashed her? Why did you threaten her with, "I'll kill you, you bitch if you tell!" Why don't you be the abusive monster you are and take credit for that black eye, for the nervous jitters that she wears, for the friends you drove away, for the tears that ran dry, for the loss of self she cannot find?

Abusers … it's time now for all humanity, on all levels, in all countries to join together to abolish you. Yes, now is the time you die. In turn, we, the world, will be free from terror.

Very truly yours,

SURVIVORS

Meet Me

Hello, meet me.
I am a survivor.
I'm the one no one notices
Or cares about.
I'm the Cinderella
Of the family
And the black sheep.
I am clad
In shields of armor
And my ears are radar.
I am always afraid
I will be hurt again
And again
With your words,
With your violent acts,
With your physical beatings,
With your sexual abuse.
Yes, you may know me.
You may know many of us.
Greet me,
For my social skills are poor.
Talk to me softly,
But, please
Don't come up behind me,
That startles me.
And, if I should speak,
Hear me,
I may stutter –
Please excuse me.
I am just beginning
To care for me.
You see ——
I don't like me.
I was always put down.
I was always wrong –
And blamed.
She said
I killed my Grandpa.
I didn't.

I didn't cry
For nearly 33 years.
I do now.
The feelings –
Emotional and Physical –
Are returning to my body.
It is scary.
Please be patient
With me.
Understand me.
I am working hard
To change.
I will not allow
Abusive behavior to continue,
Not for my family.
I am still sad, though,
For what happened to me.
It won't ever leave me.
Inside of me
I am afraid of you.
But, greet me
And you may make me smile.

Need You

I need you the most
When I am down
And say that I
Don't want you around.

I need you most
When I am low,
When seconds are passing
Oh, so slow.

I need you most
When dead is nice.
To be alive
I pay the price.

I need you most
When my sight becomes blind
And I am confused…
Which way am I moving – ahead or behind?

I need you most
Because you are my friend
And I need someone to walk with me
As I mend.

Loneliness   Sadness   Inferior   Pain

SELF-RESCUE

So many times in times of need,
As others watch but leave the scene,
A stranger from nowhere comes to our aid,
Don't want to be bothered, then just fade.
They feel useless, they can't change.
 "Can this all be rearranged?"
It's secret. No one dares to say
The fear in them says, "run away."
Run away? Keep silent! But for how long?
I know for me that abuse is wrong.
While I'm lost and really torn,
I will be strong but oh, so worn.
No one is there to help me through,
In time I'll become almost new.
I need my life given back you see,
A special oneness will become me.
To the child lost without a clue,
She sparkles now, a precious hue.
A priceless gem, unique her way,
Proves self-rescue is here to stay.

THERAPY

A different time, another place,
Pass oh so slow, this is no race.
Sometimes up, mostly down
For longer times, whatever the case.
I'm sad, I fear I'm not good enough.
I stutter, I shake, sure this is rough.
TIME, it takes time and LOTS of MILES,
Many situations, many trials.
Being in therapy sure helps a lot,
It's brain massage …tingles it's got.
"I don't know" is unaccepted,
But times I try to resurrect it.
I don't get far. I get a stare
And hands spread wide upon her chair.
So - words - the painful words come out—
Choking up, runny eyes, remember no doubt.
My memories come, no sequential order,
But all aren't good, I was not a bad daughter.
Being with mentor, she helps me feel better,
Comfortably warm, I'm so glad I met her.
She listens, she cares, she advises, she's there,
She lifts me up - not knocks me down, she's here,
For in many times of troubled days
She puts forth in many ways.
She was the Angel that came into my Life
Many years ago to help conquer this strife…
A pure role model, full of energy.
Such a great therapist, a sure necessity.

Nurturing Independence

Place me in your palm.
Lift me to your heart.
Look into my eyes.
Tell me it's alright.
Pat me on he head.
Hug me oh so tight.
Send me on my way.
Keep me in your sight.

Continue as I may.
Sometimes I trip and fall.
Now it's time to think,
Moving from the wall.
I feel your eyes upon me
Yet, I still feel very small.
The struggles that surround me,
Are oh – so very tall.

I need someone beside me
Whose words, they do not fail.
I hear them when I need them,
As I rise from 'neath a veil.
Sometimes it may seem better,
Sometimes it's gusty gales,
But if we work together,
Independence will prevail.

So Be It

So be it then I did not know
Where I did belong …
So be it then I lived in fear
Not knowing it was wrong …
So be it then their ridicule
Made me crawl within …
So be it then I was abused
But this 'twas not my sin …
So be it then I don't remember
Happy times they say I had …
So be it then, so be it now
For the past times I do feel sad …

So be it now I begin new life
Learning who I am …
So be it now my skin can feel
In some new places – yes it can …
So be it now my eyes can cry
From naught for thirty three years …
So be it now I live differently
Knowing support hears …
So be it now I search for my potential
Exploring every sign …
So be it now, metamorphosis,
I am free to fly …
This time the time is mine.

So be it now I make the changes
Needed in my life …
So be it now I persevere
No matter what the strife …
So be it now I'm taking charge
To reconstruct my family …
So be it now we learn to change
From a dysfunctional history …
So be it now undoing patterns,
Indeed, it will take time …
So be it now I'm confident
Everything will be just fine.

MINE

My Life is now mine,
It belongs to me.
I will shape it,
I will form it,
To what it ought to be.

My style is to persevere,
A winner I will be.
I'll smile with pride,
And good feelings inside,
Because I belong to me.

I don't belong to anyone
Who'll interfere with me.
I choose my wants,
I fill my needs,
Finally, I am free!

My Own Footsteps

Everyday, I wake up
And my feet, they touch the floor.
I wonder where I'm going
As I pass through the door.

These footprints, they are mine you see
So it shouldn't be a bother.
But when living in an enmeshed life,
You step on one another.

Here I go along the way
Being my own me,
'Tis strange that I approach
Today's journey differently.

So, cautiously walking forward,
Proceeding step by step,
Becoming my independent self
I'm walking my own footsteps.

To Be …

Make a Difference …
Face Your Challenge …
Take Control of Your Life …
Focus …
Secure Boundaries …
Persevere …
You Can Do It …

It is Done.

PARENTS

Parents – Praise your Children
For it is you who were their maker.
Nurture and Love Unconditionally,
Protect and Guide them through each obstacle,
Support their Dreams,
Enjoy Watching them Grow…
So, when ready, You can let them Go.

Mommy - Daddy

nurturer – physically, mentally, emotionally;
sows and reaps unconditional love, respect,
independence, self-esteem, trust,
happiness, peace, sense of self-worth.

Exhibits being a positive role model.
Counsels and guides without ridicule.
Hears words, listens, and reads body language.
Helps to be successful.
Frequently uses encouragement and praise.
Shows positive support in all situations.
Is non-abusive.
Protects.
Cares.
Is comfortable to be with –
 relaxed, trusted, safe, secure.
Cherished friend.
Shares.
Hugs a bunch.
Loves.

My Quotations

"It's when I turn you away that I need you the most"

"Some only remember what they are rather than who they are"

"Change is a Challenge"

"Don't resent telling, regret their touching"

"No more sweeping issues under the rug to fester"

"The Ocean is the where you can watch time continuously moving"

" So many of us have not reached the goals we were put on this earth to achieve."

"I learned so much about life from my pup, Baby. I Love You."

"My Pain has been too deep…
For too long…
Put there by too many who should have loved me"

"Natural is letting a spontaneous reaction happen"

"There's so much more that goes on in my head than comes out of my mouth"

"Loneliness and the feeling of being unwanted are the most terrible poverty of all."

"Live Now or Evil Won"

"Yesterdays own experiences and accomplishments.
Tomorrows own dreams and goals.
Use your yesterdays and tomorrows to guide you through all of your todays."

"Never underestimate the power of yourself"